UNSHAKEABLE: You Are Bigger Than Your Quota

Workbook

Created By: Anthony J. Williams III

UNSHAKEABLE: You Are Bigger Than Your Quota

The Official Companion Workbook

By Anthony J. Williams III

Author of *Unshakeable: You Are Bigger Than Your Quota*
Sales Leader | Executive Coach | Creator of the Unshakeable Sales System

---

This workbook is designed to help you apply, reflect, and act on every insight from *Unshakeable*. Each chapter matches the book's structure and transforms ideas into action.

Whether you're a sales rep, leader, or entrepreneur—this is your tool to build an unshakeable mindset, process, and legacy.

All rights reserved. No portion of this workbook may be reproduced, stored in a retrieval system, or transmitted in any form without prior written permission of the author.

Table of Contents

1. **How to Use This Workbook** pg. 5
2. **Unshakeable Progress Tracker** pg. 7

Core Workbook Chapters

3. **Chapter 1 – The Power of Perspective** pg. 9
4. **Chapter 2 – Who Are You?** pg. 15
5. **Chapter 3 – The Three Levers You Control** pg. 21
6. **Chapter 4 – The Sales Dance** pg. 26
7. **Chapter 5 – The Art of Listening** pg. 31
8. **Chapter 6 – Trust—The Only Currency That Matters** pg. 37
9. **Chapter 7 – The Science of Persuasion** pg. 42
10. **Chapter 8 – Handling Objections with Confidence** pg. 47
11. **Chapter 9 – Negotiation Strategies** pg. 53
12. **Chapter 10 – Solving the Puzzle** pg. 60
13. **Chapter 11 – Bad Partnerships, Bad Relationships** pg. 67
14. **Chapter 12 – Emotional Intelligence in Sales** pg. 73
15. **Chapter 13 – The Power of Storytelling** pg. 78
16. **Chapter 14 – Follow-Up: The Key to Long-Term Success** pg. 83
17. **Chapter 15 – Time Management and Productivity** pg. 89
18. **Chapter 16 – Social Selling and Digital Platforms** pg. 94
19. **Chapter 17 – Psychological Resilience** pg. 99

20. **Chapter 18 – Scaling Sales Success** pg. 105

21. **Chapter 19 – The Quote Vault** pg. 111

22. **Chapter 20 – Final Word** pg. 118

Unshakeable Workbook – Introduction & Progress Tracker

How to Use This Workbook

Welcome to the *Unshakeable Workbook*—your tactical companion to *Unshakeable: You Are Bigger Than Your Quota*.

This workbook isn't fluff. It's action. Every chapter is designed to help you implement what you read, challenge your habits, and transform how you show up as a closer, a leader, and a professional.

What You'll Need:

- A quiet space or intentional time slot (15–30 minutes per chapter)
- A journal or printed version for writing reflections
- A highlighter or colored pen for emphasis
- A willingness to be honest, bold, and unfiltered

How It's Structured:

Each workbook chapter mirrors the book chapter structure:

- **Quick Recap:** A refresher of the big idea
- **Unshakeable Insight:** One line to remember and live by
- **Reflection Prompts:** Honest, deep-thinking questions
- **Action Drills:** Tactical, repeatable exercises to build habits
- **Unshakeable Action Plan:** What to do over the next 7 days

Best Practices:

- **One Chapter Per Week:** Implement before you move on.

- **Write Everything Down:** Don't trust your mind to "remember it."
- **Go Back to Your Wins:** Revisit your work before big calls or during hard weeks.
- **Use This as a Coaching Tool:** With your team or peers for maximum accountability.

Remember: The power isn't in the page. It's in what you *do* with it.

Let's build something unshakeable.

Unshakeable Progress Tracker

Track your momentum. Mark each chapter and its action drills as you complete them.

	Chapter Title	Reflection Done	Drills Completed	Action Plan Applied
1	The Power of Perspective	☐	☐	☐
2	Who Are You?	☐	☐	☐
3	The Three Levers You Control	☐	☐	☐
4	The Sales Dance	☐	☐	☐
5	The Art of Listening	☐	☐	☐
6	Trust—The Only Currency That Matters	☐	☐	☐
7	The Science of Persuasion	☐	☐	☐
8	Handling Objections with Confidence	☐	☐	☐
9	Negotiation Strategies	☐	☐	☐
10	Solving the Puzzle	☐	☐	☐
11	Bad Partnerships, Bad Relationships	☐	☐	☐

12	Emotional Intelligence in Sales	☐	☐	☐
13	The Power of Storytelling	☐	☐	☐
14	Follow-Up—The Key to Long-Term Success	☐	☐	☐
15	Time Management and Productivity	☐	☐	☐
16	Social Selling and Digital Platforms	☐	☐	☐
17	Psychological Resilience	☐	☐	☐
18	Scaling Sales Success	☐	☐	☐
19	The Quote Vault	☐	☐	☐

Legend: ☐ = Not done | ☑ = Completed

Use this checklist weekly. Momentum loves measurement.

Unshakeable Workbook - Chapter 1

Chapter 1: The Power of Perspective

Quick Recap

Your edge isn't your product knowledge or closing script—it's your *perspective*. The ability to reframe rejection, chaos, or crisis into clarity and growth is the difference between a burned-out rep and an unstoppable force. In this chapter, we strip away ego and excuses and focus on how your outlook creates your outcomes.

Unshakeable Insight

"Perspective isn't only what you see—it's how you use it."
— Anthony J. Williams III

Reflection Prompts

1. What recent setback hit hardest, and how did you respond?

   _____
   _____
   _____

2. When have you let a negative moment define your momentum?

   _____
   _____
   _____

3. **What story are you telling yourself right now about your career? Helpful or harmful?**

   _____
   _____
   _____

4. What belief do you *know* you've outgrown but haven't let go of yet?

   _____
   _____
   _____
   _____
   _____
   _____

Action Drills

Drill #1: The Reframe Rep

Think back to a recent loss, rejection, or dry spell. Write it out in brutal honesty—what happened, how it felt.

Now: Rewrite the same moment as if it were the turning point in your comeback story.

Example:

- **Old story:** "Lost the deal, blew the pitch. I wasn't ready."
- **Reframed:** "That loss exposed a gap in my prep. I fixed it, and it became the reason I closed three deals the next month."

_____
_____
_____
_____
_____
_____
_____
_____
_____
_____
_____
_____

Drill #2: Win Lens Inventory

Create two columns:

- **Lens of Defeat**: What you see when you're in a negative headspace.
- **Lens of Ownership**: How the same scenario looks when viewed through a lens of growth.

Situation	Lens of Defeat	Lens of Ownership
Lost a deal	"I suck at closing."	"My discovery call missed the real pain. I'll ask better questions next time."
Missed quota	"I'm falling behind."	"I'm building discipline. One focused hour at a time."

Add 3 more situations from your real experience.

1. _____
   _____
   _____
   _____
   _____

2. _____
   _____
   _____
   _____
   _____

3. _____

_____

_____

_____

_____

Drill #3: Belief Burn List

Write down 3 old beliefs or thoughts that no longer serve you in sales. For each one, light a mental match:

- **Old Belief:** "I'm not good with money talk."
- **Burn It:** "I'm learning to lead pricing conversations with confidence."

Then rewrite each as an empowering belief.

_____

_____

_____

_____

_____

_____

Unshakeable Action Plan

Your Next 7 Days:

1. **Reframe one rejection** you experienced this week. Write the before/after narrative.

2. **Catch one limiting belief** in the moment and flip it with the "Burn It" drill.

3. **Track your perspective** at the end of each workday. Was it helpful or harmful? Journal 2 lines about why.

Final Thought:

You don't need a perfect market, perfect tools, or even a perfect pitch. You need an unshakeable lens. One that sees data in rejection. That finds growth in loss. That makes peace with discomfort. Because when the storm hits, your perspective is your anchor.

Let this be your mindset baseline. Everything we build from here will grow stronger because you now know the truth:

Perspective isn't what you see. It's how you respond.

Unshakeable Workbook - Chapter 2

Chapter 2: Who Are You?

Quick Recap

Before you close deals, you have to close the gap between who you are and who you're becoming. Titles fade. Quotas fluctuate. But your identity in the trenches of sales—that's what defines your edge. This chapter explores the brutal but necessary work of self-awareness and owning your role in every outcome, win or loss.

Unshakeable Insight

"You can't fix what you won't face. And in sales, consistency outshines flash every time."

Reflection Prompts

1. **What identity do you cling to most in your sales role? How does it help or hurt you?**

   _____
   _____
   _____

2. **What personal strength has helped you win deals repeatedly?**

   _____
   _____
   _____

3. **Which of your weaknesses has cost you the most money or momentum?**

   _____
   _____
   _____

4. Are you building your sales identity around approval or authenticity?

_____
_____
_____

Action Drills

Drill #1: The Brutal Self-Audit

Split a page in two columns. On the left, list your top 5 strengths in sales (e.g., rapport building, fast follow-up, storytelling). On the right, list 5 weaknesses (e.g., avoidance of price talk, rushing the close, inconsistency).

Now, beside each **weakness**, write a *single tactical habit* that would improve that area.

Example:

- **Weakness:** Avoid talking money
- **Habit:** Practice price delivery script aloud daily for 5 days

Strengths	Weakness	Habit

Drill #2: The Impostor Interrogation

Write down one belief you've had that whispers, "You don't belong here."

Answer these three questions:

- What proof do I have that this belief is false?

    o

- What wins contradict this narrative?

    o

- What would I tell a friend in my shoes?

    o

Then, rewrite your internal narrative like a coach speaking to their top performer.

_____
_____
_____
_____
_____
_____
_____
_____
_____
_____

Drill #3: Follow-Up Rescue Mission

Pick 3 leads or clients you've ghosted post-sale.

For each, draft a custom message that:

- **Owns the lapse** ("I dropped the ball"),
- **Delivers value** (tip, article, insight),
- **Opens the door** ("Let's reconnect if it makes sense.")

Send at least one today. Track what comes back.

Reference: Micro-Habit Examples

Use these as inspiration when creating your 5-day habit to overcome a sales weakness:

- **Avoiding Price Conversations:** Say your pricing script aloud 3x each morning.

- **Inconsistent Follow-Up:** Send 1 personalized follow-up before checking email.

- **Talking Too Much:** Pause 5 seconds after every prospect sentence on calls.

- **Prospecting Hesitation:** Write down 1 personal win before your first outreach.

- **Poor Time Use:** Block 20 minutes daily for focused outbound work.

Small actions, done consistently, change your sales identity at the roots.

Unshakeable Action Plan

Your Next 7 Days:

1. **Complete the Brutal Self-Audit** and post it where you work.
2. **Tackle one weakness** by creating a 5-day micro-habit.
3. **Send one Follow-Up Rescue Message** and journal the outcome.

Final Thought:

The difference between burnout and breakthrough isn't your close rate — it's your clarity. You can't outperform your identity. But you can rewire it. One decision. One habit. One moment of courage at a time.

Who are you when it gets tough?

That answer will shape your entire sales legacy.

Own your play. Own your game.

Unshakeable Workbook - Chapter 3

Chapter 3: The Three Levers You Control

Quick Recap

Sales can feel like chaos—but three things are always within your grasp: your **actions**, your **reactions**, and your **mindset**. Everything else is noise. You don't control the economy, your prospect's budget, or your competitor's discount—but you do control what you do, how you respond, and the story you tell yourself.

Unshakeable Insight

"Your actions, reactions, and mindset are the only levers you truly own. Everything else? Noise."

Reflection Prompts

1. **Which of the three levers (action, reaction, mindset) do you default to first in a crisis?**

    -

2. **Where are you overreacting to things beyond your control?**

    -

3. **What daily behavior do you know you need to own more consistently?**

    -

4. **What is the loudest negative thought you catch yourself repeating in your head?**

Action Drills

Drill #1: 50 Call Challenge – Action in Motion

Make 50 outbound touches in the next 48 hours. These can be calls, emails, LinkedIn messages, or a mix.

- Track how many you actually complete.
- Record how many replies or conversations you generate.
- Journal what happened to your confidence after completing the activity.

_____
_____
_____
_____
_____
_____
_____
_____
_____
_____
_____
_____
_____
_____
_____

Drill #2: Reaction Reset

Identify a moment this week when you felt triggered—angry, defensive, discouraged.

Write:

- What happened?
    -
- How did you react in the moment?
    -
- What could a top 1% performer have done instead?
    -
- What will you do next time?
    -

Then write out your new go-to *response phrase* to use in the heat of a challenging moment.

_____
_____
_____
_____
_____
_____
_____
_____

Drill #3: Mindset Rewire

Pick a recurring limiting thought that shows up during your sales day.

Example:

- "They're not going to pick me."
- "I'm behind—again."
- "I don't have what it takes."

Now apply the reframe:

1. **Catch It:** Identify the thought.
2. **Challenge It:** What proof do I have that this is false?
3. **Replace It:** Write your new belief (e.g., "I create value every time I show up").

Write your new belief on a sticky note, screensaver, or dry erase board.

_____
_____
_____
_____
_____
_____
_____
_____
_____

Unshakeable Action Plan

Your Next 7 Days:

1. **Pick your primary lever** this week: Action, Reaction, or Mindset.

2. **Set one habit** to strengthen that lever (e.g., 25 calls/day, reframe 1 thought/day).

3. **Track your changes** and journal the shifts you notice in performance or energy.

Final Thought:

Momentum doesn't happen by magic. It happens because someone — **you** — pulled the right lever.

You can't control what happens next quarter, but you can control how you show up this hour. You don't need perfect conditions. You need motion. You need perspective. You need the courage to pivot instead of panic.

You hold the wheel. Steer it.

Unshakeable Workbook - Chapter 4

Chapter 4: The Sales Dance

Quick Recap

Sales isn't a battle—it's a dance. And the rhythm of that dance is everything. Push too hard and you break the tempo. Move too slow and you lose the moment. This chapter is about timing, energy, and fluidity. The best closers don't overpower—they align, adjust, and guide.

Unshakeable Insight

"Sales isn't about forcing the close. It's about moving in sync with the client."

Reflection Prompts

1. When do you tend to go into "sales combat mode" instead of conversation mode?

    -

2. How well do you mirror your prospect's energy, language, and pace?

    -

3. Think of your last 3 sales calls: Were you dancing or dominating?

    -

4. What pre-call rituals do you use to find the right rhythm?

    -

Action Drills

Drill #1: Rhythm Review

Pick two recent recorded calls or virtual meetings (or reflect in detail if not recorded).

For each one, score yourself 1-10 on:

- Listening more than talking ____
- Matching their energy and tone ____
- Timing your close to their cues ____

Pattern Spotting: What behavior or moment broke the rhythm? What built trust?

_____
_____
_____
_____
_____
_____
_____
_____
_____
_____
_____
_____
_____
_____

Drill #2: Pre-Call Choreography

Before your next 3 calls, complete this short prep:

- Who is this person beyond the title? (Scan LinkedIn, social posts)
- What's their most likely pain point?
- What tone will I start with? (Warm? Direct? Curious?)
- What's the rhythm I want to keep?

Then, after each call, jot down:

- What worked?
- Where did I lose the beat?

_____
_____
_____
_____
_____
_____
_____
_____
_____
_____
_____
_____

Drill #3: Mirror & Pivot Practice

Recruit a colleague or coach. Roleplay a tough call where the prospect is:

- Aggressive
- Distracted
- Quiet

Practice:

- Mirroring their energy
- Asking a soft but insightful pivot question
- Finding an alignment instead of pushing forward

Example pivot lines:

- "Sounds like timing might be tight. What would a win look like this quarter?"
- "I get the hesitation. Definitely want to unpack where it stems from?"

Unshakeable Action Plan

Your Next 7 Days:

1. **Do the Pre-Call Choreography** for your next 3 live conversations.

2. **Rate 2 recent calls** using the Rhythm Review and write one behavior to improve.

3. **Roleplay a Mirror & Pivot drill** at least once. Journal what felt natural and what didn't.

Final Thought:

You don't win in sales by dominating. You win by dancing with precision, awareness, and trust.

When the rhythm is right, the prospect doesn't feel sold to. They feel understood.

So next time you pick up the phone or hop into a meeting, ask yourself:

Am I here to win, or am I here to move with them until they're ready to say yes?

Chapter 5: The Art of Listening

Quick Recap

Great salespeople aren't the best talkers—they're the best listeners. Silence isn't awkward. It's powerful. In this chapter, we dig into the art of listening: holding the pause, mirroring, summarizing, and asking questions that reveal the real problem behind the objection.

Unshakeable Insight

"Talk less, close more. Objections aren't roadblocks—they're gold mines."

Reflection Prompts

1. **When do you feel the strongest urge to fill the silence? What's driving it?**

    -

2. **How often do you interrupt or finish a client's thought before they do?**

    -

3. **What's one deal you lost because you listened too little or talked too much?**

    -

4. **When was the last time you uncovered a hidden problem by asking a deeper question?**

    -

Action Drills

Drill #1: The Listening Drill

For your next 3 live calls:

- Count to 5 before responding to any objection or pause.
- Write down what surfaced *only* because of that silence.
- Note your level of discomfort. Track how it changes.

Was there a change?

_____
_____
_____
_____
_____
_____
_____
_____
_____

Drill #2: Mirror, Summarize, Ask

Practice this 3-part listening formula on 3 sales calls:

1. **Mirror** the last keyword or phrase.
2. **Summarize** what you heard: "So what I'm hearing is…"
3. **Ask** an open-ended follow-up: "What does that impact look like for you?"

After each call, rate yourself: (1-5) 1= Lowest, 5 = Highest

- Did they feel heard?
    - ○
    - ○
    - ○

- Did the question go deeper?
    - ○
    - ○
    - ○

- What surfaced that wasn't on the surface?
    - ○
    - ○
    - ○

Drill #3: Counterfeit "Yes" Hunter

Review your last 5 sales conversations. Highlight every "Yes" or "Sounds good."

Ask yourself:

- Was this a **Counterfeit Yes** (stall)?

    o

    o

    o

    o

    o

- A **Confirmation Yes** (agreement)?

    o

    o

    o

    o

    o

- Or a **Commitment Yes** (decision)?

    o

    o

    o

    o

    o

Follow up with one of those prospects and ask:

"Before we move forward, what would make this a no-brainer for you?"

Track what they reveal—and whether it reopens the deal.

Unshakeable Action Plan

Your Next 7 Days:

1. **Hold the 5-second pause** in 3 live calls.

2. **Use the Mirror–Summarize–Ask method** in at least 2 conversations.

3. **Follow up on one 'yes'** that didn't turn into action. Reopen it with clarity.

Final Thought:

Silence isn't awkward—it's magnetic. Most salespeople fear the pause. The best ones use it to unlock trust, pain points, and real decisions.

You don't win by speaking louder. You win by listening deeper.

Your voice closes deals. But your ears open them.

Unshakeable Workbook - Chapter 6

Chapter 6: Trust—The Only Currency That Matters

Quick Recap

In sales, people don't buy products—they buy belief. Trust is your most valuable currency, and it's earned through honesty, consistency, and proof. One broken promise can cost you a client. One moment of truth can build loyalty for life. This chapter is about earning that trust every single day.

Unshakeable Insight

"One lie can kill your career. One truth can build an empire."

Reflection Prompts

1. **Have you ever lost a deal or client due to overpromising? What did you learn?**

   _____
   _____
   _____
   _____

2. **Where in your process are you unintentionally breaking trust—through delay, vagueness, or exaggeration?**

_____
_____
_____
_____

3. What do your clients say about you when you're not in the room?

_____
_____
_____
_____

4. Are you making it easy for clients to believe you—or hard?

_____
_____
_____
_____

Action Drills

Drill #1: The Trust Ledger

Score yourself from 1–10 across the 3 pillars of trust:

- **Honesty:** Are you transparent—even when it costs you? (__)

- **Consistency:** Do you deliver what you say, when you say? (__)

- **Expertise:** Do you bring insight and results, not just words? (__)

Circle your weakest pillar. Write one daily habit to strengthen it.

Example:

- Weakness: Consistency

- Fix: Set auto-reminders for every client follow-up.

Drill #2: The Trust Tracker (Live Activity)

For 5 client or prospect interactions this week:

- Write down what you promised

- Set a visible deadline

- Log the delivery date + any follow-up

Track whether you beat, met, or missed expectations.

- Did the client comment on it?
- How did trust shift?

Drill #3: The Honesty Script

Take one sales conversation you're prepping for. Draft a moment where you *lead with truth* instead of hype.

Examples:

- "This won't be the cheapest option—but it will be the most sustainable."
- "We're not right for every company. But if [pain point], we're the best fit."
- "I can't promise overnight results. But I can promise [realistic timeline + value]."

Deliver it in your next pitch. Journal how it shifted the energy.

Unshakeable Action Plan

Your Next 7 Days:

1. **Audit your trust pillars** and strengthen your weakest link.

2. **Track your promises** and outcomes with 5 clients/prospects.

3. **Use one Honesty Script** in a live sales conversation. Write out what happened.

Final Thought:

Trust is quiet. It's earned when no one's watching. And it compounds faster than any feature or funnel.

Sell with transparency. Show up consistently. Prove your value with facts, not fluff.

The best closers don't sell the hardest—they're trusted the fastest.

Unshakeable Workbook - Chapter 7

Chapter 7: The Science of Persuasion

Quick Recap

Persuasion isn't pressure—it's alignment. This chapter breaks down Robert Cialdini's six principles of influence and shows how to apply them authentically. When used with intention, persuasion turns resistance into trust and objections into action.

Unshakeable Insight

"Persuasion isn't about manipulating people into a sale. It's about helping them make a decision they already want to make."

Reflection Prompts

1. **Which of Cialdini's six principles do you naturally lean on in your sales process?**

    •

2. **Have you ever overused urgency or scarcity and damaged trust? What happened?**

    •

3. **Which recent deal hinged on social proof or authority to move forward?**

    •

4. **Do you believe in what you're selling enough to persuade with confidence—not desperation?**

    •

Reference: Cialdini's Six Principles of Persuasion

1. **Reciprocity** – People feel compelled to return favors or kindness.
2. **Commitment & Consistency** – People align with clear, public commitments they've made.
3. **Social Proof** – We look to others like us when making decisions.
4. **Authority** – We trust credible, knowledgeable experts.
5. **Liking** – We're more easily persuaded by those we like or relate to.
6. **Scarcity** – Perceived limited availability increases perceived value.

Use these as strategic tools—not tricks—to move people forward with integrity.

Action Drills

Drill #1: Persuasion Mapping Grid

Pick 3 deals in progress. Map which principle(s) you've used or could apply:

Prospect	Principle	Application
Acme Co.	Reciprocity	Send free audit showing value upfront
TechLift	Social Proof	Share testimonial from similar-sized client
BoldWorks	Scarcity	Mention limited onboarding slots this month

Now act on one of the mapped strategies. Track response.

Drill #2: Reframe Your Scarcity Script

Write two versions of a scarcity message:

- **Version A (Pressure-Based):** Overly aggressive or fear-driven.
- **Version B (Aligned & Calm):** Truthful, grounded in value.

Example:

- A: "This deal ends tomorrow. You'll miss out."
- B: "We have two onboarding slots left for this month—let me know if it makes sense to reserve one."

Practice the B version until it feels natural. Use it in a live call.

Drill #3: Influence in Action Story

Write out a full sales story where you used at least 3 of Cialdini's principles to win a deal.

- What did you give (Reciprocity)?
- Where did you create commitment or urgency?
- What proof or authority did you use?

Then distill the story into a 2-minute pitch version you can use in future conversations.

Unshakeable Action Plan

Your Next 7 Days:

1. **Map persuasion strategies** to 3 current deals.

2. **Use a reworked scarcity script** on one live call or email.

3. **Craft your Influence in Action story** and rehearse it as a client-facing example.

Final Thought:

True persuasion is honest, strategic, and rooted in service—not trickery.

It's how you turn "maybe" into "yes"—without ever sounding like a closer desperate for quota.

Use persuasion wisely, and you won't chase deals. Deals will chase you.

Unshakeable Workbook - Chapter 8

Chapter 8: Handling Objections with Confidence

Quick Recap

Objections aren't stop signs—they're signals. When a prospect pushes back, it means they're engaged. The worst reaction? Defensiveness. The best? Curiosity. This chapter is about responding with confidence, not resistance, and transforming "No" into a map for closing.

Unshakeable Insight

"Every objection is a chance to understand deeper—not to argue harder."

Reflection Prompts

1. **How do you usually feel when a prospect objects to your offer—threatened or challenged?**

   _____
   _____
   _____
   _____
   _____

2. **What's one recent objection that caught you off guard? How did you respond?**

   _____
   _____
   _____
   _____

3. Which type of objection triggers you the most: price, timing, or trust? Why?

_____
_____
_____
_____
_____

4. Have you ever uncovered the real reason behind a "No" and turned it into a win? What did you learn?

_____
_____
_____
_____
_____

Action Drills

Drill #1: Objection Pattern Tracker

Pick your last 5 sales calls or deals lost. For each, list:

- The objection raised
- What you said in response
- What you *wish* you had said

Look for patterns:

- Do the same objections keep coming up?
- Are your responses reactive or strategic?

Write 2 reframe scripts to improve future handling.

_____
_____
_____
_____
_____
_____
_____
_____
_____
_____

Drill #2: Objection Reframe Scripts

Choose the objection that rattles you most (e.g., "Too expensive," "We're not ready," "Already have a vendor").

Use this reframe template:

- **Validate:** "That makes total sense."
- **Uncover:** "Can I ask—what's behind that?"
- **Reframe:** "Would it help if we…"

Example:

- Objection: "Too expensive."
- Response: "Totally fair. Can I ask—how are you currently measuring ROI on a solution like this?"

- Reframe: "If we could reduce churn by 15% in 60 days, would that make the investment feel safer?"

Objection	
Response	

Reframe:

_____
_____
_____
_____

Objection	
Response	

Reframe:

_____
_____
_____
_____

Drill #3: The "No" Discovery Call

Schedule one call this week where your only goal is to uncover objections and dig deeper—not close the deal.

Start the call by saying:

"Let's assume this isn't a fit. I just want to understand what would need to change for it to make sense in the future."

Track:

- What concerns surface?
- How does their tone shift?
- What insights do you gain?

_____
_____
_____
_____
_____
_____
_____
_____
_____
_____
_____
_____
_____
_____

Unshakeable Action Plan

Your Next 7 Days:

1. **Track objections from 5 recent calls** and rewrite 2 response scripts.

2. **Roleplay your biggest objection** using the validate–uncover–reframe flow.

3. **Host one discovery call** with no close attempt—just insight collection.

Final Thought:

Objections aren't the end. They're the beginning of real sales.

Don't push back—pull deeper. Don't fear the "No"—follow it.

The best closers don't avoid objections. They mine them for gold.

Unshakeable Workbook - Chapter 9

Chapter 9: Negotiation Strategies

Quick Recap

Negotiation isn't about winning or caving—it's about *trading value*. You don't have to discount to close. You have to understand what matters most to your prospect and find a way to deliver it without compromising your worth. This chapter helps you shift from concession to collaboration.

Unshakeable Insight

"Pros don't fold under pressure. They trade value, stay calm, and close with clarity."

Reflection Prompts

1. **How do you typically react when a prospect pushes back on price—confidence or concession?**

   -

2. **What's one time you negotiated too quickly and left money on the table?**

   -

3. When have you successfully traded terms instead of lowering price? What did you offer?

   -

4. What fear still lingers around holding your line during tough negotiations?

   -

Action Drills

Drill #1: Give-to-Get Inventory

Create a two-column list:

- Column A: 5 non-monetary concessions you can offer (extended terms, onboarding support, priority access)

- Column B: What you'll ask for in return (longer contract, case study, full upfront payment)

Practice this sentence:

"We can offer [A], and in return, would you be open to [B]?"

Use this in your next negotiation.

Column A	Column B

Drill #2: The Calm Negotiator Script

Pick one deal that's currently stalled.

Write out a new outreach message that:

- Names the obstacle (price, timing, decision-makers)

- Offers one trade idea

- Reinforces your value

Example:

"I understand budget is a concern. If we structured this over two phases, would that make it easier to start? I want to make this a win on both sides."

Send it. Track the tone and traction.

_____
_____
_____
_____
_____
_____
_____
_____

_____

_____

_____

_____

_____

_____

_____

_____

_____

Drill #3: The Walk-Away Scenario

Imagine the deal you're afraid to lose.

Write out answers to:

- What's the minimum I will accept to protect my value?

- What's the one thing I won't compromise on?

- What's my confident, no-apology way to say, "I understand—it sounds like this might not be the right fit"?

Rehearse your walk-away line out loud:

"I completely respect where you're at. And I also know the impact we create isn't for everyone. If things shift, I'm here."

Unshakeable Action Plan

Your Next 7 Days:

1. **Build your Give-to-Get Inventory** and use it in a real deal.

2. **Craft and send a Calm Negotiator message** to a stalled prospect.

3. **Write your Walk-Away Scenario** and rehearse it with a peer or coach.

Final Thought:

The best negotiators don't panic. They prepare.

They walk in knowing their value, their trade zones, and their lines. They don't bluff. They don't beg. They collaborate.

Because in sales, the power isn't in the discount. It's in the clarity.

Unshakeable Workbook - Chapter 10

Chapter 10: Solving the Puzzle – Problem-Solving in Sales

Quick Recap

Sales isn't about overcoming objections—it's about uncovering the real problem and solving it with precision. Prospects rarely tell you the full story upfront. Your job is to listen between the lines, find the friction, and guide them to a better future. This chapter is about approaching sales like a puzzle—not a pitch.

Unshakeable Insight

"The best closers don't convince—they solve. And the best solutions are custom-built through better questions."

Reflection Prompts

1. Do you jump into pitch mode too quickly—or pause to fully understand the real issue?

    - Yes or No -> _____

2. What's one recent deal where solving (not selling) made the difference?

    -

3. Where do you tend to guess at the problem instead of verifying it?

_____
_____
_____
_____
_____
_____

4. How often do you ask 'What's this really about?' before offering a solution?

_____
_____
_____
_____

Action Drills

Drill #1: Objection = Opportunity Map

Think of 3 recent objections you received. For each, complete the table:

Objection	Surface Explanation	Real Root Cause	Better Question to Uncover It
"Too expensive"	Budget concern	Unclear ROI	"What return would make this worth it?"
"Bad timing"	Busy quarter	Fear of risk	"What's at stake if this continues another 3 months?"

Add one more from your own pipeline.

Objection	Surface Explanation	Real Root Cause	Better Question to Uncover it

Drill #2: Problem Discovery Playbook

Write out your personal script for uncovering pain before pitching. Use this 3-step flow:

1. **Context:** "Walk me through what's been happening recently…"

2. **Cost:** "What's this problem costing you—in time, revenue, or stress?"

3. **Consequence:** "What happens if this doesn't get solved?"

Then, rehearse it with a teammate or in front of a mirror.

_____
_____
_____
_____
_____
_____
_____

Drill #3: Solution Alignment Audit

Review your last 5 pitches.

- Did the solution address the *real* pain?

- Or did you pitch features and hope something stuck?

For 2 of them, rewrite your pitch email or summary using the following format:

"Based on what you shared about [pain point], the solution I recommend is [your offer]. Here's how it addresses [specific consequence]."

Track whether this leads to clearer follow-up or re-engagement.

_____
_____
_____

Unshakeable Action Plan

Your Next 7 Days:

1. **Map 3 recent objections** to their deeper root causes.

2. **Practice your Problem Discovery Playbook** before your next two calls.

3. **Rewrite 2 past pitches** using a solution-alignment structure.

Final Thought:

The greatest advantage in sales isn't charisma — it's clarity.

Your job isn't to sell harder. It's to understand deeper.

The closer who solves wins. Every time.

Unshakeable Workbook - Chapter 11

Chapter 11: Bad Partnerships, Bad Relationships

Quick Recap

The wrong person can cost you everything—money, time, energy, and belief in yourself. Bad partnerships, whether clients, co-founders, or internal teammates, don't just drain results—they erode your confidence. This chapter teaches you how to spot red flags, protect your energy, and walk away with strength instead of regret.

Unshakeable Insight

"Some deals aren't worth closing. Walking away is a win."

Reflection Prompts

1. **Have you ever ignored a red flag because the deal looked too good to lose? What happened?**

   _____
   _____
   _____
   _____

2. **What's one relationship you stayed in too long—client, partner, or peer?**

   _____
   _____
   _____
   _____

3. How do you personally define a healthy business relationship?

_____
_____
_____
_____

4. Do you have clear non-negotiables when it comes to who you'll work with?

_____
_____
_____
_____

Action Drills

Drill #1: Red Flag Journal

List 5 signs you've seen (or missed) in toxic clients or partners:

- Vague promises
- Dodging written agreements
- Emotional volatility
- Payment delays
- Overstepping boundaries

Now journal:

- Which red flag have you ignored the most?
- What new rule or standard will you follow from now on?

_____
_____
_____
_____
_____
_____
_____
_____
_____
_____
_____
_____
_____

Drill #2: Gut Check Matrix

Think of a current prospect, client, or collaborator who gives you mixed feelings.

Create a quick rating (1–10) for:

- Alignment with values (___)
- Communication clarity (___)
- Reliability (___)
- Respect of boundaries (___)

If the total score is under 30, write a plan to clarify expectations—or cut ties.

Drill #3: Your Exit Script

Craft a professional, no-drama message to use when you decide to walk away from a bad deal.

Use this template:

"After reviewing where things stand, I've realized this isn't the right fit for either of us. I appreciate the conversation so far, and wish you the best moving forward."

Now, identify one situation (past or present) where you *should've* used this. What would've been different?

_____
_____
_____
_____
_____
_____
_____
_____
_____
_____
_____
_____
_____
_____
_____

_____
_____
_____
_____

Unshakeable Action Plan

Your Next 7 Days:

1. **List and reflect on 5 red flags** you've seen before. Create a personal filter.

2. **Use the Gut Check Matrix** on 1 current relationship.

3. **Write and save your Exit Script.** Practice saying it out loud.

Final Thought:

Not every dollar is worth it. Not every client deserves your calendar.

The sharper your instincts, the stronger your business becomes.

Trust your gut. And when needed—walk with grace, not guilt.

Unshakeable Workbook - Chapter 12

Chapter 12: Emotional Intelligence in Sales

Quick Recap

Sales is more emotional than logical—because people are more emotional than logical. Emotional intelligence (EQ) is your ability to read the room, manage your state, and build real connection under pressure. In this chapter, we'll develop the self-awareness and empathy that separate forgettable reps from unforgettable closers.

Unshakeable Insight

"Data drives decisions. But emotion drives action."

Reflection Prompts

1. **What's your emotional state like before a big call or meeting? What do you project?**

   _____
   _____
   _____

2. **When do you struggle to regulate your emotions in sales conversations?**

   _____
   _____
   _____

3. What signs do you look for to assess a prospect's emotional state or buy-in level?

_____
_____
_____
_____

4. What does self-awareness mean to you—and how do you practice it?

_____
_____
_____
_____

Action Drills

Drill #1: Emotional Temperature Tracker

For 5 workdays, check in at three points (morning, mid-day, post-work):

- How am I feeling (1–10)?
- What triggered this?
- How did it affect my sales performance?

Use this data to identify patterns and emotional habits.

_____
_____
_____
_____
_____

Drill #2: Read the Room Log

Review 3 past calls or meetings. For each:

- What body language, tone, or energy shifts did you notice?
- Did you adjust your approach in the moment?
- What outcome followed?

Write 1 thing you'll do differently on your next call to better read and respond.

Drill #3: Empathy Builder Script

Craft a go-to response for moments when a prospect seems frustrated, anxious, or resistant.

Example:

"I can tell this feels like a lot right now. Totally fair. Want to pause and just unpack what's really top of mind?"

Write 2–3 more empathy lines in your own voice. Use one on a live call and journal the reaction.

_____
_____
_____
_____
_____
_____
_____
_____
_____
_____
_____
_____
_____
_____

Unshakeable Action Plan

Your Next 7 Days:

1. **Track your emotional state** using the Temperature Tracker for 5 days.

2. **Review 3 past calls** to assess how well you read emotional cues.

3. **Use an empathy line** in a live interaction and note the result.

Final Thought:

Emotion doesn't make sales messy. It makes it human.

The most unshakeable closers aren't just skilled — they're centered. Aware. Present. Intentional.

Lead with EQ, and you'll close with impact.

Unshakeable Workbook - Chapter 13

Chapter 13: The Power of Storytelling

Quick Recap

Facts inform. But stories persuade. In sales, logic makes them think—emotion makes them act. Great storytelling connects pain to possibility and turns your solution into a clear path to victory. In this chapter, you'll learn how to build, structure, and deliver stories that sell.

Unshakeable Insight

"People don't remember pitches—they remember how your story made them feel."

Reflection Prompts

1. What's a personal story that shaped how you sell today?

   _____
   _____
   _____

2. What client transformation have you witnessed that would make a great story?

   _____
   _____
   _____

3. Where do you tend to flood with facts instead of focusing on feeling?

   _____
   _____

4. When was the last time a story helped you close a deal—or get a second meeting?

___

Action Drills

Drill #1: Story Framework Builder

Use this 3-part framework to craft a compelling sales story:

- **Problem:** "They were facing..."
- **Pivot:** "Then we implemented..."
- **Payoff:** "Now they're seeing..."

Write 2 stories using this format:

1. A real client win
2. A transformation from your own career or team

Practice delivering both aloud in under 2 minutes.

Drill #2: Hero Shift Exercise

Pick one story you tell often (in meetings, pitches, interviews).

Now rewrite it to make the *client* the hero—not you. Focus on:

- Their challenge
- Their decision
- Their win (with your help in the background)

Use this version in your next conversation. Journal the response.

_____
_____
_____
_____
_____
_____
_____
_____
_____
_____
_____
_____
_____
_____
_____
_____

Drill #3: Story Swipe File

Create a digital note, slide deck, or doc with:

- 5 client results stories (problem → payoff)
- 3 personal credibility stories
- 2 industry-proof stories (case studies, headlines, trends)

Make this your on-demand library for prospecting, follow-ups, and proposals.

Unshakeable Action Plan

Your Next 7 Days:

1. **Write 2 stories** using the Problem–Pivot–Payoff format.

2. **Reframe a go-to story** to make the client the hero.

3. **Build your Story Swipe File** and start using it in live calls.

Final Thought:

Sales isn't a logic contest—it's an emotional connection.

Stories build that bridge. They prove your point without pressure.

Master the art of storytelling, and you'll never have to sell hard again.

Unshakeable Workbook - Chapter 14

Chapter 14: Follow-Up—The Key to Long-Term Success

Quick Recap

The close doesn't always happen on the first call. Or the second. Follow-up is where trust is built, doubts are addressed, and timing finally aligns. Most salespeople give up too early. The elite play the long game—with purpose, persistence, and personalization.

Unshakeable Insight

"Your fortune is in the follow-up. Not the pitch. Not the post. The follow-up."

Reflection Prompts

1. **How many times do you typically follow up before stopping? Why?**

   _____
   _____
   _____

2. **What's your system (or lack of one) for staying top of mind?**

   _____
   _____
   _____

3. When has a thoughtful follow-up led to a major win?

_____
_____
_____

4. Do you see follow-up as a service or as pressure? Why does that matter?

_____
_____
_____

Action Drills

Drill #1: Follow-Up Blueprint

Map out a 3-stage follow-up plan:

- **Day 1:** Recap + Thank You
- **Day 3–5:** Value drop (article, insight, resource)
- **Day 7–10:** Reconnection message ("Still feel aligned?")

Now apply it to 3 stalled deals or new prospects this week.

_____
_____
_____
_____
_____
_____

_____
_____
_____
_____
_____
_____
_____
_____
_____
_____

Drill #2: Follow-Up Language Bank

Write 5 non-pushy follow-up lines you can rotate into your emails or calls:

Examples:

- "Just wanted to make sure this didn't slip through the cracks."
- "Still makes sense to stay connected?"
- "Curious if this is still on your radar."
- "Timing's everything—want to revisit this next quarter?"
- "Not chasing—just checking in. You're still on my mind."

Save and use them on rotation.

_____
_____
_____
_____

Drill #3: Referral Follow-Up Framework

Think of 3 past clients who had a positive experience.

For each:

- Reconnect with a thank-you message
- Ask if they know someone who'd benefit from the same result
- Offer to help that referral with zero pressure

Track how many introductions come from this outreach.

Unshakeable Action Plan

Your Next 7 Days:

1. **Implement your 3-stage follow-up blueprint** with 3 real prospects.

2. **Use at least 3 different phrases** from your Follow-Up Language Bank.

3. **Reach out to 3 past clients** for referrals using your framework.

Final Thought:

Follow-up isn't annoying when it's rooted in value. It's the bridge between timing and trust.

Be the one who stays consistent. Be the one who remembers. Be the one who follows through.

Because the rep who follows up with intention wins. Period.

Unshakeable Workbook - Chapter 15

Chapter 15: Time Management and Productivity

Quick Recap

In sales, time isn't just money—it's momentum. The best closers aren't the busiest—they're the most intentional. This chapter is about reclaiming your calendar, eliminating distractions, and turning structure into your secret weapon.

Unshakeable Insight

"Discipline creates momentum. Preparation creates confidence. Time creates results—when you own it."

Reflection Prompts

1. Where are you losing the most time during the sales day?

   _____
   _____
   _____

2. Do you start your day reactively or with intention?

   _____
   _____
   _____

3. What's one activity that gives you the highest ROI—but you rarely prioritize it?

_____
_____
_____

4. What part of your day needs to be protected like gold?

_____
_____
_____

Action Drills

Drill #1: The 80/20 Time Audit

For 3 workdays, track your time in 30-minute blocks. At day's end, label each task:

- **$100/hr Task:** Revenue-generating
- **$10/hr Task:** Admin, reactive work

Tally the percentage of time spent in each.

Now answer:

- What will I eliminate?
- What will I delegate or automate?
- What will I block time for starting tomorrow?

_____
_____
_____
_____

Drill #2: Time Block Builder

Design your ideal sales day using 3–4 blocks:

- Deep Work (prospecting, calls, proposals)
- Follow-Up (emails, messages)
- Strategy/Prep (research, planning)
- Personal Recharge (breaks, reflection, growth)

Use your calendar to commit. One hour a day saved is a game-changer.

Drill #3: Distraction Detox

Pick 3 high-friction distractions (e.g., phone scrolling, unnecessary meetings, Slack chaos).

For each:

- Create a limit or blocker (e.g., app timer, calendar defense, silent mode)
- Replace it with a micro-focus habit (e.g., 25-minute sprint, 3-call challenge)

Run this detox for 5 days. Track your energy and closed deals.

_____
_____
_____
_____
_____
_____
_____
_____
_____
_____
_____
_____
_____
_____
_____

Unshakeable Action Plan

Your Next 7 Days:

1. **Complete your 3-day 80/20 Audit.** Eliminate or upgrade 3 low-ROI tasks.

2. **Build and commit to your ideal Time Block schedule.**

3. **Run a 5-day Distraction Detox.** Track how your results shift.

Final Thought:

Time is either your biggest cost—or your greatest compounding asset.

You don't need to work more. You need to work right.

Master your time, and everything else becomes easier.

Unshakeable Workbook - Chapter 16

Chapter 16: Social Selling and Digital Platforms

Quick Recap

Sales isn't just about cold calls anymore. Your online presence is part of your prospecting engine. Social selling is about visibility, value, and consistency. This chapter helps you show up strategically online, turn content into conversations, and build trust before the first meeting.

Unshakeable Insight

"Your content is your handshake. Your consistency is your credibility."

Reflection Prompts

1. How often are you creating vs. consuming content online?

   _____
   _____
   _____

2. What platform gives you the highest return—and are you maximizing it?

   _____
   _____

3. What fear or excuse has kept you from posting consistently?

   _____
   _____

4. Who do you follow that models great social selling habits? What do they do differently?

_____

_____

Action Drills

Drill #1: 30-Day Content Sprint Plan

Build a simple 4-week strategy using this cadence:

- **Week 1:** Value post (lesson, insight, story)
- **Week 2:** Case study or client win
- **Week 3:** Industry insight or myth-busting
- **Week 4:** Call-to-action (free consult, DM invite)

Outline post ideas and schedule creation time each week.

_____
_____
_____
_____
_____
_____
_____
_____
_____
_____

Drill #2: Comment-to-Conversation Flow

Identify 5 ideal prospects on LinkedIn or your preferred platform. For each:

- Leave a thoughtful comment on their post
- Wait 24–48 hours
- Send a message like: "Saw your post on [topic]—spot on. Curious to hear how you're navigating [related pain point]."

Track how many conversations start from this method.

Drill #3: Profile Positioning Audit

Review your LinkedIn or main platform bio. Score yourself 1–10 on:

- Does it speak to your ideal client's pain?
- Is your value clear in the first 3 lines?
- Is there a next step (link, CTA, contact)?

Update 3 things this week to make your profile prospect-ready.

Unshakeable Action Plan

Your Next 7 Days:

1. **Plan your 30-day content sprint.** Draft week one's post and schedule it.

2. **Engage 5 prospects** using the comment-to-convo flow.

3. **Audit and update your profile** to speak directly to your ideal client.

Final Thought:

Social selling isn't optional. It's how modern buyers vet your credibility before ever replying.

Be present. Be valuable. Be real.

Your next client might already be watching—you just need to show up.

Unshakeable Workbook - Chapter 17

Chapter 17: Psychological Resilience

Quick Recap

Rejection is part of sales—but recovery is what separates the average from the elite. Psychological resilience isn't just about bouncing back. It's about adapting, learning, and getting stronger with every "No." This chapter helps you develop the mental toughness to stay in the game and thrive under pressure.

Unshakeable Insight

"You don't build resilience by avoiding the fall. You build it by refusing to stay down."

Reflection Prompts

1. **What recent setback hit hardest, and how long did it take you to rebound?**

   _____

   _____

2. **Do you internalize rejection—or do you extract the lesson and move on?**

   _____

   _____

3. What's your current ritual for resetting after a rough day? Does it actually work?

   _____
   _____

4. How do you define resilience in your life today—and what does a stronger version look like?

   _____
   _____

Action Drills

Drill #1: Call 51 Challenge

Pick a day this week to make 50 calls, messages, or reach-outs.

- Expect rejection.
- Track each "No."
- Stay sharp until #51—then write what happened.

Journal:

- What emotions did you feel throughout?
- How did you manage the inner voice?
- What shifted by the final outreach?

Drill #2: Resilience Trigger Map

Identify 3 moments that often trigger frustration or self-doubt (e.g., ghosted email, "Not interested" reply, missed quota).

For each:

- Write the automatic thought
- Write the grounded reframe

Example:

- Trigger: "No response after a great call"
- Thought: "I blew it."
- Reframe: "Silence is neutral, not a rejection. Follow up with value."

_____
_____
_____
_____
_____
_____
_____
_____

Drill #3: Small Wins Stack

Track and celebrate 5 small wins this week:

- Follow-up sent
- Productive morning
- Client shoutout
- Courageous ask
- Clear boundary set

Write down each win and how it made you feel. Stack these to create momentum.

_____
_____
_____
_____
_____
_____
_____
_____
_____
_____
_____
_____
_____

Unshakeable Action Plan

Your Next 7 Days:

1. **Complete the Call 51 Challenge.** Track how your mindset shifts.
2. **Map 3 emotional triggers** and create your grounded reframe.
3. **Log 5 small wins** and reflect on the confidence they build.

Final Thought:

Resilience isn't built in the win. It's built in the *recovery*.

You will get knocked down. But the question is: will you get back up smarter, stronger, and more focused?

Refuse to retreat. Rise instead.

Unshakeable Workbook - Chapter 18

Chapter 18: Scaling Sales Success

Quick Recap

Success is great. Repeatable success is unshakeable. This chapter is about transforming wins into systems, momentum into processes, and hustle into scalable habits. Whether you're a solo rep, team leader, or business owner—scaling starts with structure.

Unshakeable Insight

"If you can't repeat it, you can't grow it. Build a system. Not just a streak."

Reflection Prompts

1. **What's a sales win you've struggled to repeat? Why do you think that is?**

   _____
   _____
   _____

2. **Do you have consistent systems—or are you winging it deal to deal?**

   _____
   _____
   _____

3. Which part of your process is the most chaotic? (Outreach, discovery, follow-up, etc.)

_____
_____
_____

4. What could you automate or delegate to buy back your time?

_____
_____

Action Drills

Drill #1: Sales System Snapshot

Map your current sales process across key stages:

- Prospecting
- First contact
- Discovery
- Proposal
- Follow-up
- Close

For each, write:

- What tools or steps you use
- Where things break down
- What can be improved or templatized

Pick one weak area to optimize this week.

Drill #2: Daily Huddle Template

Design a 15-minute daily self-check or team sync format:

- Wins from yesterday
- Pipeline top priorities
- Blocks or bottlenecks
- Today's action plan

Use this rhythm for 5 days and note the momentum shift.

Drill #3: Replication Playbook

Pick one successful close in the last 30 days. Break it down:

- Where did the lead come from?
- What made them trust you?
- What process or message clicked?

Now turn that into a step-by-step sequence or checklist. Use it as your new mini-playbook for future deals.

_____
_____
_____
_____
_____
_____
_____
_____
_____
_____
_____
_____
_____
_____
_____
_____

Unshakeable Action Plan

Your Next 7 Days:

1. **Map and optimize one weak spot** in your sales system.
2. **Run your Daily Huddle template** for 5 straight days.
3. **Create one Replication Playbook** based on a recent win.

Final Thought:

Winning once is exciting. Winning over and over again—without burning out—is unshakeable.

Success at scale isn't louder. It's more precise. More repeatable. More structured.

Systems scale what hustle starts.

Unshakeable Workbook - Chapter 19

Chapter 19: The Quote Vault

Quick Recap

Words matter—especially when they strike at the right time. Quotes can act as anchors, mantras, or mindset reset buttons when sales feels like chaos. This chapter is your curated vault of the most impactful lines from the book and beyond—paired with reflection, application, and intention.

Unshakeable Insight

"You don't rise to your quota. You rise to your standard."

Reflection Prompts

1. **Which quote from this book shook you the most—and why?**

   _____
   _____
   _____

2. **What words do you return to when things feel heavy or uncertain?**

   _____
   _____

3. Do you use affirmations or mantras in your daily sales rhythm? Why or why not?

_____
_____
_____

4. What one quote will you live by this quarter—and what would living it *look* like?

_____
_____
_____

Action Drills

Drill #1: Quote Reflection Journal

Choose 10 quotes from this book (or the curated list below). For each, write:

- What it means to you

- When it applies most (emotionally or situationally)

- What action it inspires

Use one per week for the next 10 weeks as your anchor.

Drill #2: Weekly Quote Challenge

For the next 4 weeks, pick one quote per week:

- Write it at the top of your weekly planner

- Say it aloud each morning

- Use it to reset when doubt creeps in or challenges spike

Track your mental state and outcomes weekly.

_____
_____
_____
_____
_____
_____
_____
_____
_____
_____

Drill #3: Create Your Personal Quote

Craft a one-line mantra that captures your current mission.

- What truth do you need to hear daily?

- What standard do you want to rise to?

- What would your future self say in your toughest moment?

Write it. Post it. Speak it.

_____
_____
_____
_____
_____
_____
_____
_____
_____
_____
_____
_____
_____
_____
_____

Unshakeable Quote Bank (Starter List)

1. "You don't need perfect conditions. You need motion."

2. "Objections are gold mines, not grenades."

3. "The best closers listen louder than they speak."

4. "Consistency over intensity wins every time."

5. "Time is your most underused advantage."

6. "You are not your quota. You are your standard."

7. "Give value. Then give more."

8. "Every deal is a mirror. What you bring is what reflects."

9. "Push through the call you're dreading. It holds your next win."

10. "Prepare like you're broke. Pitch like you're the best."

_____
_____
_____
_____
_____
_____
_____
_____
_____

Unshakeable Action Plan

Your Next 7 Days:

1. **Reflect on 10 quotes** and journal their impact using Drill #1.

2. **Commit to a Weekly Quote Challenge.** Start with the one that hits hardest.

3. **Write your own quote.** Use it as a mantra for your next sprint.

Final Thought:

When your strategy falters, return to your standard. When doubt creeps in, return to your words.

Because your mindset sets the ceiling for your momentum.

And sometimes, the right line at the right time can change everything.

Final Word: Your Unshakeable Sales Legacy

Chapter 20: Final Word

You made it.

Not just to the end of a workbook—but through 19 chapters of reflection, grit, application, and growth.

This workbook wasn't about learning more—it was about doing more with what you already know. About owning your next move and becoming unshakeable in a world that often rewards quick wins and shallow tactics.

You chose a different path.

You built a new lens in Chapter 1. You wrestled with objections in Chapter 8. You mapped systems in Chapter 18. You anchored your mindset with the Quote Vault in Chapter 19.

Each page, each drill, each reflection has been a rep—strengthening your confidence, your resilience, and your ability to close with clarity, integrity, and power.

What Happens Now?

You don't need another chapter. You need momentum.

Revisit this workbook. Use it as your sales journal. Bring it to team huddles, coaching sessions, and quiet moments where doubt tries to creep in.

This isn't a one-and-done tool. This is your **sales playbook for the long game**.

And if you're wondering...

- "Am I really built for this?" — You are.

- "Can I rise when pressure hits?" — You will.

- "Will this work if I actually work it?" — Without question.

You're not just chasing quota anymore.

You're building a legacy.

One that isn't shaken by rejection, market shifts, or missed quarters.

Because when your process is unshakeable—**you are, too.**

Keep going. Keep growing. Keep showing up.

See you at the top.

— **Anthony J. Williams III** *Author of Unshakeable: You Are Bigger Than Your Quota*

www.ingramcontent.com/pod-product-compliance
Lightning Source LLC
Chambersburg PA
CBHW082210070526
44585CB00020B/2355